sacred
goodbyes

honoring and healing
your pain and loss

eileen dunn

Robert D. Reed Publishers • San Francisco, California

Robert D. Reed Publishers
750 La Playa Street, Suite 647
San Francisco, CA 94121
Phone: 650/994-6570 • Fax: 650/994-6579
E-mail: 4bobreed@msn.com
Web site: www.rdrpublishers.com

Designed and typeset by Katherine Hyde
Cover designed by Julia A. Gaskill at Graphics Plus

ISBN 1-885003-61-7

Library of Congress Control Number 00-102826

Produced and Printed in the United States of America

for Linda,
who catches me when I am falling . . .
and who, somehow, always knows my heart . . .

for Kevin
he is she as she is he
I miss you so much, my compadre . . .
who knew you were going to teach me
so much about death?

contents

When a death occurs, it is often our Spirit, our Human Spirit, that moves us through the devastating pain and helps us reconnect with Life. It is a loving power that guides us through our darkest dark. § The following is written from the heart. § It is written for all who go through the grieving process. Even though every situation is unique, the path of grief is universal in nature. When a loved one dies, we all go through a common journey. § I pray that I have captured the pain of our journeys so that together we can find our way back to the joy of living our lives on this beautiful planet. § It is a work of deep sorrow. It is a work of finding incredible peace.

It is our journey.

. . . and

the world

shatters

he wakes up—
brushes his teeth—
he greets the day—
rents movies.

and then there is an accident,

a terrible, terrible accident.

and, in a flash,

he
is

GONE.

he no longer walks the Earth.

he no longer wakes up.
he no longer brushes his teeth.

he
is

DEAD.

one second, here . . .

the next second, there.

I cannot comprehend this.
I cannot accept this.

I do not know how to believe this.

what I do know is,
I just want to be with him.
I just want to be with him . . .

I need to be near him.

I have to be with him.
I need him.

~ ~ ~ ~ ~ ~

where has he gone?
when will he be back?

~ ~ ~ ~ ~ ~

with one sentence
the world

SHATTERS.

"I regret to inform you…"

suddenly,
All is dark.
All is pain.
All is cold,

and "normal" will never be the same.

oh, dear God,
I ache . . .
I can hardly take a breath.
I can hardly move.

~ ~ ~ ~ ~ ~

how do I accept
the Unacceptable?

~ ~ ~ ~ ~ ~

eyes swollen.

burning tears.

sobs from the core-of-your-being.

heart shattered and broken.

mind numb.

body aching.

can a person
really
LIVE
through this?

~~~~~~

is there anything worse
than identifying
A BODY
in the morgue?

~~~~~~

... and the world shatters

how do we
choose the clothes
for you to wear in your casket?

do we dress you in your Sunday best,
complete with belt and matching shoes?

or do we dress you in more casual,
comfortable attire?

do we bring several outfits,
and let the undertaker decide?

how do we go to your closet
and choose the clothes
for you to wear in your casket?

how do we actually do this?

HOW?

I look at you
in the casket
and I know you are only sleeping.

WAKE UP!

this bad joke is over.
please get out of that box.
I'm tired of this,

and I need everything to get back to normal.

come on, get up.
I've seen you asleep
hundreds of times.

and this looks no different.

GET UP. GET UP. GET UP!!!

before I take off my shoes
and get into that box with you.

please . . .

. . . and the world shatters

they put our

~ ~ ~ ~ ~ ~

Beloved

~ ~ ~ ~ ~ ~

in the ground.

and then we go eat…

how do we do this without

losing

our

MINDS?

oh my God!
there is a headstone
with your name on it—

how did this happen?
this is **not** my idea
of the way things should be—

this is not my way.

I am so angry

at you,
for leaving me.

at myself,
for not saving you.

I am so angry

at God,
for calling you Home.

come back,
stay with me.
come back,
please don't go.

I need you.

dear God,
please give him back.

why do you think
you can just swoosh him away?

who do you think
you are, God?

DEATH . . .

final . . .

final . . .

final . . .

EXIT.

sacred goodbyes

what Purpose has been
served by this death

?

~ ~ ~ motions.
going through the motions.

it's as if I am a robot,
I'm in a dense and suffocating fog.

conversations that I'll never remember.
as soon as a sentence is spoken,
the thought is lost.

~ ~ ~ food.
eaten or forgotten,
all tasting like dust,
tasteless and waxen.

my deepest memory of those dreadful days
is entering into the dark abyss of the void . . .

and slowly,
ever so slowly,

I am overwhelmed
by an excruciating understanding
of the finality of death
on
earth.

~ ~ ~ ~ ~ ~

he isn't coming back, is he?

~ ~ ~ ~ ~ ~

I'm waiting
for him to walk into the room
and fix dinner,
his favorite dinner of spaghetti.

his shoes are near the door,
just waiting for him
to put them on.

we are all
just waiting for him.

anxiously . . .
waiting . . .
waiting . . .

just waiting for him to come home
and fix spaghetti.

your Light has gone out
and you have left your body.

my
soul
cries,

"WHY?"

sacred goodbyes

I scream your name
at the top of my
lungs—

but you
do not
answer.

we were supposed to grow old together.
remember our plans?

~ ~ ~

a pair of rocking chairs on the porch . . .
raising chickens and selling their eggs . . .
having a mango tree . . .

we were going to move to a small house
in a remote corner of the world . . .

~ ~ ~

broken
dreams,
shattered
hopes.

will I ever be able to form a new plan?

pain is my
        constant
            companion

one of the most difficult aspects
of this process
is that
I have never hurt so deeply,
and it's you that I need to talk with.
it's you that could help me through this.
you have been there for me,
always.
but not this day,
when I want you the most.
when I need you the most.
you are not here.
you are
gone,
for death has called you away.

far,
far,
away.

I am

                  alone.

so very

                  alone.

there is nowhere to go.

there is no place to escape.

I cannot take this,
every cell in my body
shouts.

I **truly** cannot take this.

I am
going
CRAZY.

I am slowly and definitely losing my mind.

and
yet,

nobody seems
to be listening.
nobody seems
to notice.

I am alone,
so very

alone.

I can't see through this fog . . .
I can't seem to remember anything.

did I eat?
did I pay the electric bill?
did I return that phone call?

I just can't seem
to see through this fog.
it weighs heavily upon my body.

I get confused
easily.

I get upset
often.

I ache
deeply.

**I keep looking for a
lighthouse.**

sacred goodbyes

eat.
but the food tastes like dust.

dress.
but I don't even know
if it's winter or summer.

hold a conversation.
but I can't think straight
and I don't know what day or month it is.

answer the phone.
but I can't speak.

take a walk.
but my body is too heavy.

share a meal with a friend.
but the thought of food makes me sick.

listen to music.
but it only bangs in my ears.

take a nap.
but I only cry.

the pain of missing is too deep.
I can only sit,
and on occasion . . .

blink my eyes.

why have you
left me here?

why have you
left me alone?

why have you
left me without warning?

~ ~ ~ ~ ~ ~

did you know you would take my soul?

~ ~ ~ ~ ~ ~

now, what am I supposed to do?

time has lost its meaning,
for my perspective has changed.

has it been one month?
six months?
or was it yesterday?

I can no longer
discern a monday,
a tuesday, a
wednesday, or a
thursday.

my life has become a series of days
that I have somehow made it through,
one breath at a time.

days that seem to stand still.
but, in the end,
the restless sleep came.

how long will this ache last,
this open, oozing wound?

I do not know the answer to this question,

but now I take it
one breath at a time.

you came to me in a dream,
a dream so real.

I could touch you.
I could hold you.
I could feel you.

"what's it like being dead?"
I asked.

"I don't know, I haven't accepted it yet,"
you told me . . .

how do you begin to say good-bye?
what is this "letting go" I hear of?

I've watched him
grow to be a wonderful person.
I've laughed with him countless times
when he was at his silliest.

I've watched him
fall and make stupid mistakes.
I've cried with him as he picked up the pieces.

and, through it all
I've loved him
with all of my heart,
and all of my soul.

his presence in my world
has filled me
with powerful love,
sweet laughter
and true friendship.

how do I begin to say good-bye?

I cannot do this without you.
this life . . .
this journey . . .
this trip on Earth . . .

do you hear me?
I cannot do this without you . . .

I can't.
I won't.
I quit.
I sleep.

I wake up.

and I find
that I have no choice
but to do this
without you,

this life,
this journey,
this trip on Earth.

sacred goodbyes

for some incomprehensible reason,

a reason
I cannot see
or understand,

I am required
to do this without you.

to live this life,
to experience this journey,
to take this trip on Earth.

I carry you within my heart.
I honor your life through mine.

wait for me, my gentle friend.
my time will come
to join you.

for now,
I am busy
with my life,
my journey,
and my trip on Earth.

~ ~ ~ ~ ~ ~

a heart
that is given permission
to feel everything
sure can get
a bad headache on occasion.

~ ~ ~ ~ ~ ~

sacred goodbyes

the grief process is heart-wrenching for
every person
who goes through it.

*some people grieve
in silence.*

*some people grieve
through anger.*

some people grieve
by withdrawal,

others, by denial.

do not compare grief processes.

All Are Valid.

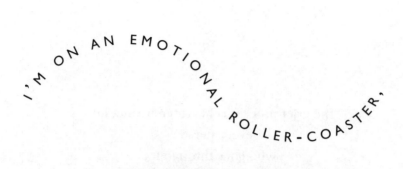

I'M ON AN EMOTIONAL ROLLER-COASTER,

and I don't know how to get off.

one moment,
I'm okay.

the next moment,
I'm a basket case.

up and down,
up and down,
up and down,

in and out,
in and out,
in and out,

around and round,
around and round.

where do I buy a ticket for a canoe ride?

sacred goodbyes

~ ~ ~ ~ ~ ~

a gentle voice told me,
"you will get through this."

a gentle pair of arms
held me and reassured me,

even though all was not well,
all still was . . .

~ ~ ~ ~ ~ ~

pain is my constant companion

pictures
just aren't enough.

I don't need a picture to remember
your intense passion for life,
your amazing creativity,
your gentleness.

the picture does not capture
your sense of humor,
your intelligence,
your deep appreciation of our world.

the picture
cannot eat salsa with me.

grief
chooses us.
we do not
wake up one morning
and call out,

"oh grief, I have something to learn.
feel free to enter my life
and teach me of your wonders."

oh no!
grief chooses us . . .

one second changes everything.
one second can shatter our souls.
in one split second, our world crumbles.

oh no . . .
we do not invite grief in—

~ ~ ~

she barges.

~ ~ ~

I ache for you.

a physical gnawing of the soul.

all of me hurts ...

especially my heart,
but definitely my soul, too.

this has brought me
to a new dimension of pain—
a pain so consuming
that every breath I take hurts.

and there is nothing I can change.

all I can do
is sit.

all I can do
is feel.

I feel sick,
nauseated with disbelief.

but there is nothing I can do,

except sit.

just

sit.

~ ~ ~ ~ ~ ~

sometimes,
it's just one breath at a time.
one long, deep breath at a time.

~ ~ ~ ~ ~ ~

forever young.

do you know you will be forever young
in my mind?

you will never grow old—
you will never grow old . . .

you are now
forever young.

oh God!
not Christmas!

why do I hate the holidays so much?

since I was young,
I had always liked Christmas,
every single one.

I had loved the holidays.
my memories speak of happy times.

but now,
just the thought of Christmas
makes me want to run and hide.

I need to go away at Christmas time.

is it because you are not here and it is so obvious?

is it because of all the Christmases that we shared,
or
is it because it takes too much energy
to have a semblance of a "normal"
holiday?

have I lost my holiday spirit ... forever?

sacred goodbyes

for now,

I just close
my eyes
and
silently
count the
days
until the
end of the
holiday
season.

all I know
is

BAH HUMBUG.

journey to the core

I was having a horrible, horrible day,
a day beyond description.

the anguish I was feeling made it
impossible for me to take a breath.

my heart was heavy and my breathing shallow.

the weight on my heart was smothering,
and I did not know what to do.

I was the only one home,
so I went to my room
and lay on my bed in the fetal position.

I was engulfed in darkness.

I never knew it was possible to feel this much pain.

as I was lying there,
I had the thought,

"follow your pain."
I was unclear as to what this meant.

"follow your pain, do not try to block this. go with this.
let go and follow your pain."

and suddenly,
my consciousness shifted,

I was *inside* my body,
experiencing life from a
completely different perspective.

it was as if my consciousness
was being pulled forcefully
through many tunnels.

I was being hurled at great speeds,
deeper, deeper inside.

somehow, I was traveling
through time and space.

I remember thinking,

*"oh my god. what if I get stuck?
what if I get lost here? what if I die from this?"*

deeper and deeper. faster and faster.

I could not stop where I was going.
I could not control where I was going.

sacred goodbyes

I was just *falling* through space.

I was traveling to a Universe,
a Universe deep within me.

I passed through limitless galaxies.
I encountered numerous planets
in various star systems.

everything was a **blur.**

I saw only blackness.
I knew only coldness.
I was afraid,
and I was dying.

this travel was too much.

I was steadily losing my life-force.

I could actually feel my life-force
draining from me.

suddenly
a great **"WHOOSH"** went through my being.
I shuddered and completely let go.

I had surrendered.

just when I really thought I was going to die,
another shift happened.
I had never come close to experiencing anything
like this on Earth.

I found myself in Another Place. a place of peace.
a place surrounded in gentleness.
a place of pure peace, pure gentleness.

Light was everywhere.

I was embraced by the Light.
I was comforted by the Light.
I was filled with the Light.

I was warm and I was safe.

I truly had found peace.

I truly had found the Light,
and all was perfect.

I felt such quiet and tenderness.

in a flash of a moment,

I knew I was loved.
I knew I had found hope.
I knew I had found Life.

I had traveled to the core of Life,
and I found immeasurable comfort.

I cannot tell you
how long I was there,
maybe moments,
maybe hours.

what I can tell you,

this gift of healing I received
is with me forever.

I now **know** there exists
a place of Great Love and Eternal Life.
my doubts have left me.

the healing process has begun . . .

beginning
to dry
the tears

my "unseen friends," my angels
are working overtime
to get me through this.

this I know,
because, when I am very quiet,

I hear them
gently whispering.

I feel them
sending me love,

and peace fills me.

is there a heaven?

perhaps I do not know how
to envision this—

but I seem to know
without doubt—

yes, there is a heaven.

forget the words.
there are no words.

this pain needs a hug,
a sincere,
loving,
kind hug.

**forget the words,
and remember to hug.**

~~~~~~

wherever you are,
I know you know,
I send you my love.

~~~~~~

sacred goodbyes

the journey of grief
is **not** a journey any person would choose.

and yet, we all find ourselves walking that path,
taking that journey.

a path of loss,
too great to comprehend.

a path filled with pain,
beyond measure.

it is a journey of sorrow
and choking, suffocating grief.

and yet,
somehow,
along the way,
it becomes a journey of acceptance,
of glimpses of peace,
and "letting go"
to the ways
of God.

and quiet, quiet

surrender.

one second changes everything.
one decision leads to your death.

if you hadn't gone there,
if only you had stayed home,
if you had watched that second movie . . .

or is it a much different Picture than that?

has it always been known
by the angels and God
that *this* would be
your moment to return
to them?

was your death, like your birth,
already destined?

this seems to be the Truth
of this mystery of Life and Death.

I find great comfort in this.

it sure doesn't mean I like it,
but I do find comfort in this.

I read the obituaries now.
they have a new meaning for me.

yesterday, I read about a lady
who lived to be 101 years old.
on that same day,
a girl died from cancer at 11 years old.

the length of time we have
on our planet
can never be known.

what we do know is the "now" of life.
this moment,
this precious, precious moment.

this moment that is ours
to live.
to experience.
to love and be loved.

because we do know
our journey on Earth is over
far too quickly—
even if we live
to be
101.

I reached a point
when I couldn't take it anymore.
when I knew I could not go on.

I was without hope,
without energy,
without feelings.

one day I looked around
and I saw others who walk this planet,

and gradually,
ever so tenderly,
I invited them

back into my world,
back into my heart.

I began to feel again
ever so slowly,
ever so gently,

and my heart opened
cautiously,
and my soul sang
quietly . . .

I pray for the courage
to stay focused in my day-to-day living,
so that I may fulfill my Destiny.

I pray for that deep Peace,
the peace that is beyond understanding,
so that I may find Comfort here.

I pray for Faith,
that living, dynamic energy
so that I may embrace each day.

I pray for Acceptance.

I pray for you.
I pray for me.
I pray for others
in the same situation as I am.

I pray.

I heard a joke
today.

and I laughed ...
I actually laughed ...

it felt so right.
it felt so life-affirming.

I actually laughed.

the wonderment of life
flowing through me
filled me.

I had thought
that I
would
never
ever laugh
again.

I have come to understand,
this pain is with me always.
it does not leave my heart,
I can get in touch with it at any moment.

I have come to understand
that I may also experience
joy and lightness.
I can still share friendship and laughter.

I embrace both
overwhelming pain and magnificent joy,

in the same heart,
at the same time.

my body hurts
and so I take a bath.
a long, hot bath.

actually,
this has become a daily ritual,
my daily "quiet time."

I fill the tub with
very warm water and lots of bubbles.
I put in some aromatherapy oils.

I let the water heal me.

I let the water soothe me.

sometimes,
I read.
sometimes,
I pray.
sometimes,
I cry.

but I really do find
that this quiet time
of bubble baths and aromatherapy
helps me cope.

~ ~ ~ ~ ~ ~

do you watch my dreams
from where you are?

~ ~ ~ ~ ~ ~

sacred goodbyes

there is no way around the pain
on an anniversary,
a birthday
or a special day . . .

I have learned
to accept that this is inevitable.
I accept this and take
extra care of myself.

perhaps, I take the day off,
or take a long walk.
maybe I'll get a massage,
or call a special friend.

I eat well.

I take it slow that day,

honoring,
in my own way,
both
Life and Death.

when I least expect it,
I am once again
engulfed in dark despair.

it may be a fleeting memory
that calls me.

it may be one of your favorite foods
that triggers this.

it may be a movie we saw together,
an anniversary,
a graduation,
a beautiful sunset.

I have learned
to experience fully the anguish,
knowing it will pass eventually,

and then, my love for you fills me,
and I am okay.

gifts

along

the way

you have sent me rainbows,
and I know they are a gift from you.

two years in a row,
once on your birthday,
and another time,
on the anniversary of your death.

oh, I was having such a difficult day,
and amazingly,
even when the sun was shining,
you sent me a rainbow.

it was calming for me
to hear from you.
it was necessary for me
to hear from you.

**I thank you
for the rainbow.**

do not worry,

I will find you,

across all time boundaries,
through different dimensions,
wherever you are.

do not worry.
I will find you.

I will never lose you.

I know you too deeply.
I love you too dearly.

I will return to you,
always.

our connection is eternal.

because of our relationship,
I am a better human being.

a relationship filled
with love and friendship,
anger and forgiveness,
growth and exploration,
joy and pain.

I am "more" because of our relationship.

I understand your love of the Earth,
and you have taught me deep respect
for her magnitude.

I felt your passion.

I looked into your eyes and saw God.

I have been blessed,
eternally blessed,
through our relationship.

*deep gratitude to you,
my gentle friend.*

dance
this dance of life with me,
a dance of movement and measure,
love and friendship.

sing
a song of soul with me,
a song full of freedom and promise,
joy and laughter.

dance this dance of life with me.

when one of us is called by death,
we will have our connection
and our love
and we will not lose each other.

oh, dance this dance of life with me.

~ ~ ~

as I move
consciously and painstakingly
through my pain,

I honor you.

as I live my life
joyfully and lovingly,

I honor you.

as I remember
my destiny
and fulfill my purpose here,

I honor you.

~ ~ ~

there is no easy path
through the grief process.

each experience is uniquely different.

there are no "time limits,"
no magical wand
that can erase the pain.

the journey is filled
with anguish,
devastating loss,
and isolation.

reality becomes confused,
our lives have been broken.

it's easy to forget
the people
now in your life.

begin to remember them.
remember to hug them.
remember to love them.
remember to share with them.

**we are all in this,
together.**

~ ~ ~ ~ ~ ~

say
"I love you"
as often as you can.

these small words
will bind you together
for eternity.

~ ~ ~ ~ ~ ~

I now hug
a little longer.

I now notice
life-force everywhere.

I now experience
so many more feelings.

I have let down
some of my walls.
(actually, they shattered themselves
when **all** was
shattered.)

I have become
more vulnerable,
more open,
more passionate,
more alive.

I know of my love
for this planet.
I know of my commitment
to be here, now,
fulfilling my destiny.

I often eat chocolate-chip cookies
hot from the oven.

sacred goodbyes

I have come to know peace
by accepting your death.

in order to reach this peace,
I have had to re-evaluate all of my beliefs
and search my soul from the inside out.

I have traveled
to the darkest dark,
the loneliest lonely,
the deepest deep.

I have traveled
alone . . .

I have known shock,
anger,
confusion,
hopelessness,
and deep depression.

I have known blackness,
cold, numbing blackness.

I hate this reality—
the reality of your death.

I have fought against it—
I have raged against it.
I have done it all.

and then I began to listen.

I listened very closely.
I listened very intently.

I heard.

I heard words of love,
of acceptance.
of peace.

I felt myself being guided
through the darkest dark.

I can only say,
my helpers were from beyond
this dimension.

I was visited in dreams,
and I came to believe
you are well.
and you are happy.

our connection is eternal.

~ ~ ~ ~ ~ ~

by accepting Death
I accept Life.

~ ~ ~ ~ ~ ~

and now
for the rest
of your life

the news continues to be absorbed.

the funeral has been planned
and is now over.

so many people
have come
to share their
support and love.

the flowers are gone,

the Kleenex put away.

the phone calls are minimal.

and, **oh my God!**

all you see is black.
all you feel is pain.
all you know is anguish.

what
now?

you are in uncharted territory here
and your life has changed.

how will you go about your days?

think carefully about this.

be gentle with yourself.

do not rush
to get back to "normal."

do not push
to get "done with this."

take all the time you need.

and be kind to yourself.

be very kind.

you will live through this experience.
as difficult and as crushing as it is,

you will live.

you will wake up
in the morning,
and face the rest of your life.

you are now at a fork in the road.

the path you take is your choice.

will you embrace Life
and all its experiences?

or will the pain cause you
to deny Life and close down?

your decision is essential.

we are talking about
the quality of your life,
the quality of your days.

you still have your life . . .
this we know.

there are many others
in your world . . .
this we know.

your life has been
deeply affected . . .
this we know.

exactly how this death
will permanently affect your life
and your relationships with others,
lies in your hands and in your heart.

listen deeply to your soul.

nature is waiting to soothe you.

so many different colors,
so many beautiful sunsets,
so many opportunities to walk in the rain.

remember, the colors in nature
are of a frequency that your body
will find healing.

remember to remember nature.

look to the stars
and wonder of eternity.

look to the plants
and wonder of growth.

watch the seasons,
and understand the cycles of
birth and death.

watch, just watch,
and absorb.

let go of the need to know *"why?"*

the workings of God are beyond our
understanding.

when you let go,
peace fills your heart,
acceptance fills your heart,
and love fills your heart.

you have entered the healing process.

take care of yourself.

I mean, really take care of yourself.

**treat your body with
kindness and gentleness.**

take time for yourself.

eat nutritiously.
drink pure water.
take walks.
watch the butterflies.

bake cookies.
share an iced tea with a friend.
see a funny movie.
wear comfortable shoes.

listen to your favorite music
and dance! dance! dance!
take a lavender bubble bath.
draw something.

get body work done on a regular basis.
call old friends.
watch the sunsets.
walk in the rain.

and remember to buy some
malted milk balls.

begin to do the things that help you
feel alive
and fill you with contentment.

remember, you can know
both sadness and happiness
in the same heart.

take small steps.

and above all,

be comfortable.

making the choice to heal
is a powerful, powerful choice.

this will give permission
to all of your seen and "unseen" friends

to come to you,
to guide you along your way,
and to love you completely.

when you invite your healing,
peace will enter your being,
love will enter your heart,
and joy will fill your world.

this may not happen overnight
but it will happen.

yes, healing will happen.

there is no getting around the
emptiness and the void.

what we must find
is a way to live through this.

as you call upon your memories
of your beloved,

let this energy heal you.

as you connect with your beloved
on levels beyond this dimension,
let this teach you of eternity.

as you move through your pain
you will know glimpses of peace,

and perhaps, quiet acceptance.

I wake up.

I brush my teeth.

I greet the day.

I rent movies.

and
I embrace this day as it unfolds.

I am so happy for this day.
I am so happy to be here, now.

I know this
as I smile with the hummingbird
as she buzzes near the lilac bush.

~~~~~~

and out of the cocoon
emerges a

butterfly.

~~~~~~

sacred goodbyes

my beloved soul family,

as we walk this devastating road
of deep sorrow and grief,

we all begin to remember
we are one.

may your journey
know Love.
may your journey
know Peace.
may your journey
reveal your Purpose.

in gentleness,
eileen

Books Available From Robert D. Reed Publishers

Please include payment with orders. Send indicated book/s to:

Name:_____

Address:_____

City:_____ State:_____ Zip:_____

Phone:(____)_____ E-mail:_____

Titles and Authors	Unit Price
Conscious Divorce: finding freedom through forgiveness by Eileen Dunn	$9.95
Sacred Goodbyes: honoring and healing your pain and loss by Eileen Dunn	9.95
Gotta Minute? How to Look & Feel Great! by Marcia F. Kamph, M.S., D.C.	11.95
Gotta Minute? Practical Tips for Abundant Living: The ABC's of Total Health by Tom Massey, Ph.D., N.D.	9.95
Gotta Minute? Yoga for Health, Relaxation & Well-being by Nirvair Singh Khalsa	9.95
Gotta Minute? Ultimate Guide of One-Minute Workouts for Anyone, Anywhere, Anytime! by Bonnie Nygard, M.Ed. & Bonnie Hopper, M.Ed.	9.95
A Kid's Herb Book For Children Of All Ages by Lesley Tierra, Acupuncturist and Herbalist	19.95
House Calls: How we can all heal the world one visit at a time by Patch Adams, M.D.	11.95
500 Tips For Coping With Chronic Illness by Pamela D. Jacobs, M.A.	11.95

Enclose a copy of this order form with payment for books. Send to the address below. Shipping & handling: $2.50 for first book plus $1.00 for each additional book. California residents add 8.5% sales tax. We offer discounts for large orders.

Please make checks payable to: Robert D. Reed Publishers. Total enclosed: $_____. See our website for more books!

Robert D. Reed Publishers
750 La Playa, Suite 647, San Francisco, CA 94121
Phone: 650-994-6570 • Fax: 650-994-6579
Email: 4bobreed@msn.com • www.rdrpublishers.com